© **POSITIVE MANTRAS FOR YOU**
BY SANDEEP RAVIDUTT SHARMA

Table of Contents

Introduction IV

Positive Mantras For You................... 1

© **POSITIVE MANTRAS FOR YOU**
BY SANDEEP RAVIDUTT SHARMA

Introduction

This book provides you with a list of **100 motivational quotes and thoughts** focussing mainly on improving your wellness quotient. Start your day with positive thoughts and you can experience the world of happiness. Your choice of words would decide whether at the end of the day you will listen to wind chimes or spend further time in collecting the ashes. The happiness one derives is amazing when ideas turn into reality. It's much bigger and deeper than the success itself.

I'm sure if you keep reading, referring, sharing these thoughts and quotes, you may derive inspiration and develop a good understanding of various perspectives and facts about life.

"Share the words of encouragement and it becomes Positive Mantras for the world."

I sincerely hope, you will find this book amazing, interesting, rejuvenating, unique and constant source of inspiration.

Thank You and Happy Reading.

© POSITIVE MANTRAS FOR YOU
BY SANDEEP RAVIDUTT SHARMA

© Copyright 2018 Sandeep Ravidutt Sharma - All rights reserved.

In no way is it legal to reproduce, duplicate, or transmit any part of this document in either electronic means or in printed format. Recording of this publication is strictly prohibited and any storage of this document is not allowed unless with written permission from the publisher. All rights reserved. The information provided herein is stated to be truthful and consistent, in that any liability, in terms of inattention or otherwise, by any usage or abuse of any policies, processes, or directions contained within is the solitary and utter responsibility of the recipient reader. Under no circumstances will any legal responsibility or blame be held against the author / publisher for any reparation, damages, or monetary loss due to the information herein, either directly or indirectly. The author own all copyrights.

Legal Notice:
This book is copyright protected. This is only for personal use. You cannot amend, distribute, sell, use, quote or paraphrase any part or the content within this book without the consent of the author or copyright owner. Legal action will be pursued if this is breached.

Disclaimer Notice:
Please note the information contained within this book is for motivational, educational and knowledge sharing purpose only. Every attempt has been made to provide the reader accurate, up to date and reliable complete information. No warranties of any kind are expressed or implied. Readers acknowledge that the author is not engaging in the rendering of legal, financial, medical or professional advice. By reading this document, the reader agrees that under no circumstances the author / publisher is responsible for any losses, direct or indirect, which are incurred as a result of the use of information contained within this document, including, but not limited to, —errors, omissions, or inaccuracies.

If you have further questions, contact on
Tel: +919969256731
Email: sandeepraviduttsharma@gmail.com

© **POSITIVE MANTRAS FOR YOU**
BY SANDEEP RAVIDUTT SHARMA

Dedication

This book is dedicated to **Goddess Bhairavi**. In the Hindu religion, the Goddess Bhairavi represents divine anger and wrath which is directed towards impurities within us as well as to the negative forces that obstructs our spiritual growth. Bhairavi Mata is also called as **Shubhamkari** and does good things. She is often depicted in images as holding a book, rosary and making abhaya and varada mudra with her hands. She is fiercely protective, lending us wisdom and power, steadiness and clarity. She personifies light and fire, supporting us to reveal what we keep hidden and inviting us to explore our hidden mind and any secret darkness.

I hereby recite the following Bhairavi mool mantra...
"Om Hreem Bhairavi Kalaum Hreem Svaha"
And pray to **Goddess Bhairavi** for lending wisdom and power, steadiness and clarity in the life of my readers and the world. May Goddess Bhairavi protect us from negative forces along with removing impurities of our mind.

POSITIVE MANTRAS FOR YOU

© **POSITIVE MANTRAS FOR YOU**
BY SANDEEP RAVIDUTT SHARMA

The single seed is the mother of billion of trees. Become the seed of knowledge, and you can illuminate the path of billions across the world.

© **POSITIVE MANTRAS FOR YOU**
BY SANDEEP RAVIDUTT SHARMA

Success eludes those who don't use Today in the hope of stocking Tomorrow. Use your efforts today to bring home Success.

© **POSITIVE MANTRAS FOR YOU**
BY SANDEEP RAVIDUTT SHARMA

Your credibility comes to the fore when you have no wealth to show.

Get ready to receive your dues. Good news is about to knock your door.

Don't just look at the pain and sufferings. Also, pay attention to the hands that are helping and lifting the fallen souls from drowning.

© **POSITIVE MANTRAS FOR YOU**
BY SANDEEP RAVIDUTT SHARMA

Don't damage your relationship with the war of words.

Centuries have passed, but we are still learning how to maintain peace and harmony.

The act of kindness doesn't need any language to express.

© **POSITIVE MANTRAS FOR YOU**
BY SANDEEP RAVIDUTT SHARMA

Never talk to anger and wait for calm to return home.

Freedom of mind is more precious than the physical one.

© **POSITIVE MANTRAS FOR YOU**
BY SANDEEP RAVIDUTT SHARMA

Spend time with yourself if you really want to know what you want from life.

© **POSITIVE MANTRAS FOR YOU**
BY SANDEEP RAVIDUTT SHARMA

God makes the way but cannot walk on your behalf.

Dreams fall apart when action is missing. Dedicate your efforts with complete focus and achieve your dreams.

Attract all kinds of positivity in your life by remaining optimistic irrespective of the results.

Yesterday you have decided, today you have to act.

© **POSITIVE MANTRAS FOR YOU**
BY SANDEEP RAVIDUTT SHARMA

When you don't get what you want. You blame God and question his existence. It would be better if you question yourself and try to understand your own shortcomings responsible for your downfall.

Attract positive thoughts by reading inspirational stories, by meeting achievers and conditioning your mind to filter negativity right at the entry level.

Help...while others are thinking

The future is always perfect for those who ensure Today is bright and satisfying.

Do things which you like Don't bother about the world.

© **POSITIVE MANTRAS FOR YOU**
BY SANDEEP RAVIDUTT SHARMA

Don't break the rules unless you are convinced that it's obstructing the growth path.

The day you realise the importance of discipline you will grow.

You can't beg or buy happiness. But you can apply the brake and say bye to sadness by staying positive.

Hiding the truth guarantee sleepless nights. Reveal it in the right way and you can have peace of mind.

© **POSITIVE MANTRAS FOR YOU**
BY SANDEEP RAVIDUTT SHARMA

Get ready to receive the best in life NOW.

It's your smile which introduces you to the world of happiness.

© **POSITIVE MANTRAS FOR YOU**
BY SANDEEP RAVIDUTT SHARMA

Get down at the right station if you intend to board a connecting train from there.

One can only promise his best for the day. Tomorrow never comes.

Don't talk when you can deliver in that time.

Yesterday you failed but took away precious life lessons. Today you were the winner because you made the attempt to remember those lessons and avoided mistakes.

© POSITIVE MANTRAS FOR YOU
BY SANDEEP RAVIDUTT SHARMA

You cannot have things or people in your life forever, whether you like it or not.

Somebody has rightly said...Do whatever you love and Love whatever you do.

Time is running. Whether it is fast or slow your mind decides.

Cheer for those who are making attempt to win.

© **POSITIVE MANTRAS FOR YOU**
BY SANDEEP RAVIDUTT SHARMA

Sometimes it's nice to get defeated if your intentions are noble enough to allow others to also succeed and gain confidence.

Sleep as if there would be no tomorrow.

© **POSITIVE MANTRAS FOR YOU**
BY SANDEEP RAVIDUTT SHARMA

Barriers in life appear at every stage. All you need is grit and determination to cross over all such barriers.

Get familiar with the environment or make it familiar with you.

Those who are counseled by time need no further advice to do the right things in life.

Do not wait for people to validate when you are on the side of truth.

Time only waits for those who have mastered the art of going ahead in time with a firm eye and control on the present.

At times you don't know whether you are right or wrong. Keep the patience, and time will decide it for you.

© **POSITIVE MANTRAS FOR YOU**
BY SANDEEP RAVIDUTT SHARMA

It's your mind which makes you believe and achieve. You need to feed the dose of positivity to your mind, and you can win.

Give a chance to those who have failed and rejected to start afresh.

The world awaits your performance on the big stage. Prepare yourself for this event; you are here to win.

Pursue your dreams if you remember it well after waking up from sleep.

Try to change your attitude and imbibe positive traits. The world around you would change within minutes.

God wants you to lead, so please come forward and hold the reins of your life and those connected to you.

© POSITIVE MANTRAS FOR YOU
BY SANDEEP RAVIDUTT SHARMA

Thoughts keep visiting you every nanosecond. It is useful for you and others only if it is captured or noted and shared through different modes. You never know the thought which you may have shared have visited someone thousands of years ago or will reappear again in the future. In my view, thoughts are always around us. It's just that it has matched our frequency and get captured and delivered. We may think it's original or something exclusive...But it always existed and not just got created now...

It's your confidence which shows you the way to go.

© **POSITIVE MANTRAS FOR YOU**
BY SANDEEP RAVIDUTT SHARMA

Fix your mind on the present, and you can do wonders for the future.

God has gifted you the heart of Gold. If you have realised this, I'm sure no one who is helpless would go empty handed from your door and kindness would rule.

Don't shy away from your responsibility of being human.

Instead of making attempt to scale Everest, it's wise and kind to touch the ground and help the downtrodden.

Those who want to forget their gloomy path should not be questioned more about it. It can affect their present also. Help them to bury their past by drawing them to the present.

Struggle in life is not one time and test you throughout.

Change is the way of life. Be the change, and you can control it.

Appreciate others, not with the intention of getting it back in return.

When you become the voice of the crowd, it means you are on the road to leadership.

Throw away all those things and memories of your life which doesn't motivate you.

Those who prefer, sleepover Karma don't need a calendar.

Time paints life in a combination of black and white and you start losing hope or start the blame game. Keep the patience, and you will find life playing with true colours of joy and happiness.

© **POSITIVE MANTRAS FOR YOU**
BY SANDEEP RAVIDUTT SHARMA

Attitude makes you what you are today.

Escape from the trap of negativity by staying positive and committing to creativity.

Loud words often make people act deaf. Speak the right words in a gentle tone if you want to evoke the right response.

Do different things in a unique way to promote or bring consistency in the process and execution.

© **POSITIVE MANTRAS FOR YOU**
BY SANDEEP RAVIDUTT SHARMA

When you earn due to hard work of others, do give them their due share and you can grow richer.

You had enough rest, now is the time for a power packed performance. Get Going...

© **POSITIVE MANTRAS FOR YOU**
BY SANDEEP RAVIDUTT SHARMA

You spend a lifetime to build a dream home and feel happy about it ultimately. When you help others in their quest to build a good life, you feel happier.

You can't force someone to bless you. Blessing comes automatically from a person who is happy with your deeds. It's a natural emotion which cannot be forced or bought. Keep doing good things in life, and you can live a blissful life.

Your smile in the morning adds magic to my day. Thanks to Mother Nature.

When efforts follow your dream, the success cannot turn a blind eye and is sure to meet you.

© **POSITIVE MANTRAS FOR YOU**
BY SANDEEP RAVIDUTT SHARMA

Never force your love and likeness on anyone. Give them space and wait for their response.

Those who win your heart are your friends.

Creativity stems from a calm mind.

© POSITIVE MANTRAS FOR YOU
BY SANDEEP RAVIDUTT SHARMA

You may not like what everyone says, but that doesn't mean you should quit. Keep Going...

Changing your appearance can make you feel happy temporarily. But positive influence on your mind can make you happy forever.

You have the power to write your own story.

© **POSITIVE MANTRAS FOR YOU**
BY SANDEEP RAVIDUTT SHARMA

You can't change your past. But in case it was ugly you can make an attempt to shine in the present with your determined and focused approach. Someday these golden layers would cover the ugly ones.

Sharpen your skills regularly and be ready to deliver your best on any day.

God always loves you whether or not you remember him.

You don't have to wait for someone's order if your efforts are directed towards improving the world.

Your thousands of excuses can't convince someone who practices and accepts only truthful conduct.

Success loves passion. And passion comes from your involvement. Your involvement is the result of positive affirmation and motivation.

The day we stop hating each other in the name of religion, caste, colour or language, heaven would descend on earth. Be human.

One tiny step to resolve now can prevent a bigger conflict later.

Finding more success can hardly satisfy your craving for love. Love comes when you can find inner peace and share the joy outside.

Smoke never appears on its own. It always comes on the invitation of fire. The fire ignited by someone with ill intention can destroy. Light the fire of love and knowledge to illuminate the world.

Even when you do nothing, things move forward. It is because, time never stops for anyone.

Be the crusader rather than the invader.

© **POSITIVE MANTRAS FOR YOU**
BY SANDEEP RAVIDUTT SHARMA

The to-do list can be effective if the one who created it remembers to refer.

Be a Sky when it's time to accommodate and save many.

Parents are the most precious and greatest gift of the creator to the Mankind.

© **POSITIVE MANTRAS FOR YOU**
BY SANDEEP RAVIDUTT SHARMA

The vastness of the Sea inspires one and all. The kindness of the Sea reflects in its act of giving shelter and nourishment to the millions of beings within.

Get ready to pray at least for your well being and those of your near and dear ones. Prayer has the power to heal, attract happiness and bring in calmness and contentment in your life.

Taking the blame on self and not pointing fingers to others when one loses a game is the hallmark of a gentleman for whom the spirit of the game is above all.

Success changes its face every now and then. Today it's someone else, Tomorrow it can be you. Keep going with a smile.

Silence is Golden. You can communicate thousands of words just by remaining silent. But remember silence practiced at the wrong time can signify your weakness and your inability to raise your voice when required.

Don't argue if you want to make other people understand. First, listen to the perspective of the other person and then put your point.

The colours of joy keeps changing depending on the mood of the individual. Train your mind to attract joyfulness and calmness.

www.ingramcontent.com/pod-product-compliance
Lightning Source LLC
Chambersburg PA
CBHW070803220526
45466CB00002B/528